SING, PRECIOUS MUSIC

A collection of twentieth-century choral works
for mixed voices
selected by Barry Rose

CONTENTS

NOVELLO

Notes by Barry Rose

Bernard Rose · Feast song for Saint Cecilia
(Recording: St. Paul's Cathedral Choir. Hyperion CDA66439)
This collection takes its title from the refrain of Bernard Rose's *Feast song for Saint Cecilia*, written for the 1975 St. Cecilia Festival Service in the church of St. Sepulchre-without-Newgate, in the City of London, where it was sung by the combined choirs of Westminster Abbey and St. Paul's Cathedral, under the direction of Douglas Guest.

For a text, the composer asked his son, Gregory, to write a suitable poem, and it not only features trumpets, organs, strings, horns, harps and flutes, but also the waking hours of each day, from sunrise, 'midday heat', through to 'cool evening breezes'. The musical result is most memorable and moving, and could be described as a master-class in word painting. From the opening 'great flashes of grandeur' (bars 3-4) through to 'lulling her people to calm rest' (bars 75-78), there are deft touches of skill, highlighting every facet of the text, with each verse followed by a recurring and haunting treble solo in each of the three refrains.

Bernard Rose was Organist and Informator Choristarum at Magdalen College, Oxford, 1956-81.

Derek Bourgeois · Harvest Anthem
(Recording: Guildford Cathedral Choir. Guild Music GMCD 7110)
For the academic year 1968-69, Derek Bourgeois joined the music staff at Cranleigh School, Surrey, and during that time, he agreed to write a piece for the 1969 Guildford Diocesan Choirs Festival, held in nearby Guildford Cathedral.

As the conductor of the Festival, I suggested that we might take a fresh look at Harvest, since there seemed to be a shortage of both words and music for suitable choral pieces, and it was to a colleague, in Cranleigh Preparatory School, that the composer turned for a suitable poem. Ian Freegard's inspired words bring some of the practicalities of harvest time, from jam-making ('the plum and wasp'), fishing ('great nets spawn silver into trawlers' hulls'), and even brewing ('the cannery and brewery are working round the clock') through to the traditional elements of thanksgiving at harvest festivals ('the marrow and the sheaf-shaped loaf'), culminating in a paean of praise in thanks 'for blessed ripeness You have sent', where, in the organ pedal part, the composer quotes from the traditional harvest hymn *We plough the fields and scatter.*

From the joyfully rhythmic opening bars, Derek Bourgeois catches every mood of the poem with unerring skill. The mechanical throb of the cannery and brewery is brilliantly captured, whilst the hushed chordal writing perfectly mirrors the reverence of the text at 'The honoured altar-bread and chaliced wine', as well as in the final petition 'that all may share in your harvest of plenty'.

Derek Bourgeois was Musical Director of The National Youth Orchestra of Great Britain, and Director of Music at St. Paul's Girls' School, London.

Gerald Hendrie · There is no rose
(Recording: St. Albans Abbey Choir. Lammas Records LAMM 81)
Dating from 1981, this 4-part unaccompanied setting was written for a specific occasion, and the sound of a specific choir. The occasion was the first broadcast of the Advent Carol Service from the chapel of St. John's College, Cambridge, and the sound that the composer had in mind was the sound of George Guest's choir at St. John's, in which the composer's sons, Piers and Dorian, were choristers.

The anonymous macaronic text comes from a fifteenth-century manuscript in the library of Trinity College, Cambridge, known as the Trinity Roll (MS 0.3.58), and to it, the composer has set flowing melodic lines, introducing the voice parts in contrasting musical textures in verses 1 and 2. Elsewhere, the text is highlighted by a change of key and imitative writing in all parts, whilst the ending returns to the original musical theme in the home key of F major, with an effective and extended setting of 'Transeamus' (let us go over – i.e. may we follow).

Gerald Hendrie was Organ Scholar at Selwyn College, Cambridge, and later Professor of Music at The Open University.

Arthur Wills · The praises of the Trinity
(Recording: Ely Cathedral Choir. Herald Records HAVPCD 197)
From the opening quasi-fanfare style of the first few bars, it is obvious that here is a piece for a very special occasion – in this case, the 1964 enthronement of The Right Reverend Edward Roberts as Bishop of Ely. The text is peculiar to Ely, (the Cathedral is dedicated to the Holy and Undivided Trinity) and at previous enthronements it had been said, in a responsorial form, as the new Bishop entered the Cathedral at the beginning of the service.

For the 1964 enthronement, Arthur Wills, who was then organist at Ely, was asked to write this setting for his choir to sing, unaccompanied, at the back of the nave. The splendour of the occasion is immediately captured in the first phrase, followed by a joyfully animated rhythmic pattern for the upper voices ('May the Blessed Godhead of the Father...'), answered in a responsorial fashion by the altos, tenors and basses, after which all voices join together to sing the same rhythmic patterns, in unison. The composer graphically paints the text at 'perpetual glory', and rounds off the piece with the slower and triumphantly declaimed 'throughout the everlasting ages'.

Arthur Wills was Organist and Master of the Choristers at Ely Cathedral from 1958-90.

Sebastian Forbes · Gracious Spirit, Holy Ghost

(*Recording: Guildford Cathedral Choir. Lammas Records LAMM 87*)
Written for the wedding of two friends, Sebastian Forbes sets four verses from Bishop Christopher Wordsworth's extended paraphrase of I Corinthians 13, in a subtle and individually harmonic style. Scored mainly for unaccompanied five-part choir, the lilting 5/8 writing is later embellished with some florid and delicate organ interludes that seem to give an impression of the fluttering wings of a dove, depicted as the Holy Spirit at Christ's baptism (Mark 1, v. 10), on which the final verse ('From the over-shadowing Of thy gold and silver wing') is based.

Sebastian Forbes was Professor of Music at Surrey University from 1981-2006.

Christopher Robinson · Rejoice and be merry

(*Recording: St. George's Chapel Choir, Windsor. Guild Music GMCD 7105*)
Scored for 6-part unaccompanied choir, here is a jaunty and rhythmic look at a traditional text that dates from the days of the West Gallery village musicians in the county of Dorset. Christopher Robinson's writing is concise, vocally memorable, and always responsive to the text. The more 'adventurous' chords at the end may raise a few eyebrows amongst those of listeners who have been used to the simple traditional setting to these words!

Christopher Robinson was Organist and Director of Music at Worcester Cathedral, St. George's Chapel, Windsor, and St. John's College, Cambridge.

Herbert Howells · I love all beauteous things

(*Recording: Wells Cathedral Choir. Hyperion CDA67494*)
Robert Bridges' poem dates from 1890, and more than eighty years later, Herbert Howells was to make an incognito visit to St. Albans Abbey, to absorb the atmosphere and acoustics of the building, in preparation for writing his 1977 setting of these words. The choice of text was particularly appropriate to a forthcoming exhibition in the Abbey, entitled *The Hands of the Craftsman*, and the result is one of Howells' most sumptuous and affecting choral works. From the choir's ardent and impassioned first phrase, the work moves through a succession of rich and memorable moments, demonstrating the mature and chromatic harmonic style in what is one of the composer's last choral works.

In this edition, we have sought to clarify the composer's indications over the use of the organ pedals (the original was printed on two staves).

Herbert Howells was Professor of Composition at the Royal College of Music for over fifty years.

Simon Preston (arr.) · I saw three ships

(*Recording: The choir of St. Thomas' Church, New York. Pro Organo CD 7200*)
The origin of the text of this well-known carol remains obscure, but it is thought to have some connection to the Shrine of the Three Kings in Cologne Cathedral, reputedly containing relics belonging to the Magi, and originally in Constantinople.

For many years, it has been sung to this well-known traditional English melody, and Simon Preston's individually styled arrangement dates from 1965, whilst he was sub-organist at Westminster Abbey. The traditional-style opening, over a gentle and sustained chordal organ accompaniment, gives way to some divided part-writing for the upper voices above some chromatic harmonies in the lower parts.

New interest is introduced with later changes of key, and in verse 7, where the melody apparently disappears, it can be tracked, being quickly passed from one part to another, in groups of four notes. The joyfully effervescent ending is heightened by the use of running passages in the organ part.

Simon Preston is a former Organist and Master of the Choristers at Christ Church Cathedral Oxford, and Westminster Abbey, London.

Grayston Ives · Let all the world in every corner sing

(*No commercial recording yet available*)
In 1973, Grayston Ives was commissioned to write an extended choral piece for the Guildford Festival, to be sung as the final item in a concert in Guildford Cathedral where, at the time, the composer was a tenor lay-clerk. Intimately knowing the sound of the choir, the organ, and the building, he chose a festive text by George Herbert to reflect the occasion, and set it in an extended and exciting way.

The first notes of the short organ introduction set the mood of exhilaration, and this is immediately mirrored by the opening choral entries. From bars 13-22, the repeated short and offset settings of the word 'sing' bring more life to the text – the offset entries vividly painting 'in ev'ry corner sing'. The repeated motif 'My God and King' from Herbert's poem is musically heightened by the composer initially setting it in a cumulative fashion, adding one word at a time in verse 1 (see bars 28-36), until the complete phrase is joyously declaimed.

Contrasted with this are delicately fashioned phrases, with legato lines set against busy semi-quavers (bar 38 onwards, *et al*), and imitative and quiet entries (bar 70 onwards), building from there to an impressive and sustained climax.

Grayston Ives is Organist and Informator Choristarum at Magdalen College, Oxford.

Composed for the 1975 Festival of Saint Cecilia in the church of St. Sepulchre, Holborn, London

Feast song for Saint Cecilia

Gregory Rose (b.1948)

Bernard Rose (1916–96)

* An exact reduction of the vocal lines is not shown at all times.

nine trum-pets blaz - ing at her side, glides_____

nine trum-pets blaz - ing at her side, glides_____ o - ver

nine trum-pets blaz - ing at her side, glides_____ o - ver

nine trum-pets blaz - ing at her side, glides_____ o - ver

____ o - ver sea____ and land____ rous - ing voi - -

sea____ and land____ rous-ing great or - gans and voi - -

sea____ and land____ rous-ing great or - gans and voi - -

sea____ and land____ rous-ing great or - gans and voi - -

accel. - - - - Faster ♩ = 80

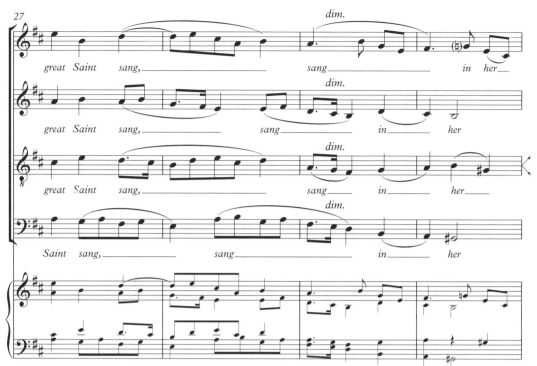

6

and ur - ges him to do great____ things, great____ things.____

and ur - ges him____ to do great____ things, great____ things.____

ur - ges him____ to do great____ things, great____ things.____

- ges him to do great____ things, great____ things.____

SOLO

____ Sing,____ sing pre - cious mu - sic, sing to the Cre-

Sing pre - cious mu - sic,

Sing____ pre - cious mu - sic,

Sing____ pre - cious mu - sic,

When cool eve - ning bree - zes calm_____ wea - - - ry

- ning bree - zes calm_____ wea - - - - - - ry

When cool eve - ning bree - zes calm_____ wea - - - ry

- ning bree - zes calm_____ wea - - - - ry

folk, in - vit - ing them_____ to rest, Ce - ci - lia, Ce -

folk, in - vit - ing them_____ to rest, Ce - ci - lia,

folk, in - vit - ing them_____ to rest, Ce - ci - lia,

folk, in - vit - ing them_____ to rest, Ce - ci - lia,

* If the upper D is sung, the A must be omitted.

Harvest Anthem

Ian Freegard (b.1926)

Derek Bourgeois (b.1941)
Opus 30

The can - ne - ry and bre - we - ry

The can - ne - ry and bre - we - ry

The can - ne - ry and bre - we - ry are work - ing round the clock, are

The can - ne - ry and bre - we - ry are work - ing round the clock, are

are work - ing round____ the_ clock, are work - ing round____ the_

are work - ing round____ the_ clock, are work - ing round____ the_

work - ing round the clock, are work - ing round the clock, are work - ing round the

work - ing round the clock, are work - ing round the clock, are work - ing round the

clock, are work-ing round the clock.

clock, are work-ing round the clock.

clock, are work-ing round the clock.

clock, are work-ing round the clock.

The hon-oured al - tar-bread and chal-iced

wine with grate-ful glow are set be-fore the Kind - ly One who planned this

now _____ up-on our har-vest - sha - ven fields, ___

now _____ up-on our har-vest - sha - ven fields, ___

now _____ up-on our har-vest - sha - ven fields,

now _____ up-on our har-vest - sha - ven fields, ___

The win - dow plants, _____ the dah-lias in cot - tage

The win - dow plants, _____ the dah-lias in cot - tage

The win - dow plants, _____ the dah-lias in cot - tage

The win - dow plants, _____ the dah-lias in cot - tage

thanks for bles - sed ripe - ness_____ You_____

have sent._____

for Dr. George Guest, Dorian Hendrie and the choir of St. John's College, Cambridge

There is no rose

Words: anonymous 15th century

Gerald Hendrie (b.1935)

for the enthronement of the Bishop of Ely, May 9th, 1964

The praises of the Trinity

Words: traditional

Arthur Wills (b.1926)

e - ven to Fa - ther, Son and Ho - ly Spi - rit,

e - ven to Fa - ther, Son and Ho - ly Spi - rit,

e - ven to Fa - ther, Son and Ho - ly Spi - rit,

e - ven to Fa - ther, Son and Ho - ly Spi - rit,

who mak - eth the whole world sub - ject to his Law.

who mak - eth the whole world sub - ject to his Law.

who mak - eth the whole world sub - ject to his Law.

who mak - eth the whole world sub - ject to his Law.

Hon - our, might and power and em - pire be un - to the

Tri - ni - ty in U - ni - ty, to the U - ni - ty in Tri - ni - ty:

through-out the e - ver-last-ing a - ges.

through-out the e - ver-last-ing a - ges. To the Tri - ni - ty be e - ver-

through-out the e - ver-last-ing a - ges. To the Tri - ni - ty be e -

To the U - ni - ty be per - pe - tu - al

To the U - ni - ty be per - pe - tu - al

- last - ing light,_____ be e - ver -

- ver - last - ing light,_____

glo - ry, be per - pe - tu - al glo - ry, glo - ry, glo - ry, glo - y:

-ty be per - pe - tu - al glo - ry:

-ty be per - pe - tu - al glo - ry:

-ty be per - pe - tu - al glo - ry:

through - out the e - ver - last - ing a - ges.

through - out the e - ver - last - ing a - ges.

through - out the e - ver - last - ing a - ges.

through - out the e - ver - last - ing a - ges.

Specially composed for the wedding of Michael Pearce and Margaret Humphrey Clark,
St. George's Church, Ashtead, Surrey, Marth 16th 1968

Gracious Spirit, Holy Ghost

Bishop Christopher Wordsworth (1807–85)

Sebastian Forbes (b.1941)

19

But the great - est of the three,

Join - ing hand in hand a - gree; But the great - est of the three,

Join - ing hand in hand a - gree; But the great - est of the three,

But the great - est of the three,

But the great - est of the three,

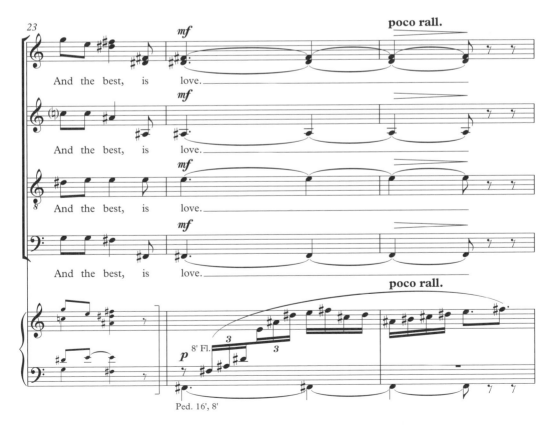

23

And the best, is love.

And the best, is love.

And the best, is love.

And the best, is love.

poco rall.

8' Fl.

Ped. 16', 8'

Rejoice and be merry

Words: anonymous

Christopher Robinson (b.1936)

-wise a bright star in the sky did ap-pear which led the wise men from the

East_ to draw near. mm_____

They found the Mes-si - ah, sweet Je - sus our King, who

trea-sures un - fold,_ myrrh, in - cense and gold. So bless-ed for

trea-sures un - fold,_ myrrh, in - cense and gold. So bless-ed for

trea-sures un - fold,_ myrrh, in - cense and gold. So bless-ed for

- fold, and_ un - to him of - fer'd myrrh, in-cense and gold. So bless-ed for

- fold, and_ un - to him of - fer'd myrrh, in-cense and gold. So bless-ed for

e - ver be Je - sus our King,_ who brought us sal - va - tion, his_ prais-es we'll

e - ver be Je - sus our King, who brought sal - va - tion, his prais-es we'll

e - ver be Je - sus our King, who brought sal - va - tion, his prais-es we'll

e - ver be Je - sus our King,_ who brought sal - va - tion, his_ prais-es we'll

e - ver be Je - sus our King, who brought sal - va - tion, his prais-es we'll

50

Composed for a Special Festival Service held in conjunction with the 'Hands of the Craftsman'
Exhibition in St. Albans Abbey as part of the 1977 'Festalban' Festival

I love all beauteous things

Robert Bridges (1844–1930)   Herbert Howells (1892–1983)

I love_____ all beau - teous things,_
I love_____ all beau - teous things,_
I love all beau - teous things,_

___ I seek_____ and a - dore them;_____
___ I love and a - dore_____ them;_____
___ I seek_____ and a - dore____ them;_____
I seek_____ and a - dore____ them;_____

poco accel.   **Poco più vivo** ♩ = c.72, *still*

Come primo

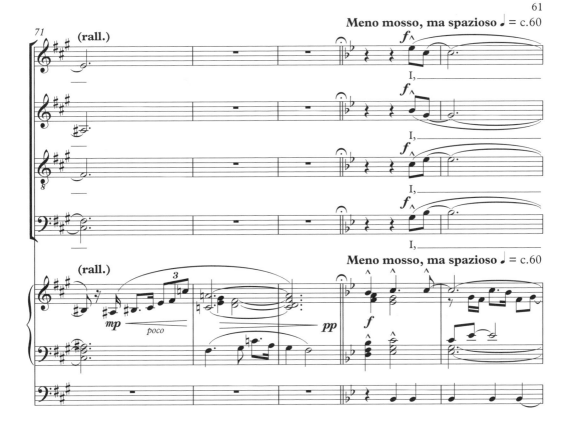

I saw three ships

Words: traditional

arr. Simon Preston (b.1938)

what was in those ships all three? On Christ-mas Day in the morn - ing.

SOLO

3. Our

Sa - viour Christ and his la - dy, On Christ-mas Day, on Christ-mas Day, Our

mp

Ped.

Sa - viour Christ and his la - dy, On Christ-mas Day in the morn - ing.

dim.

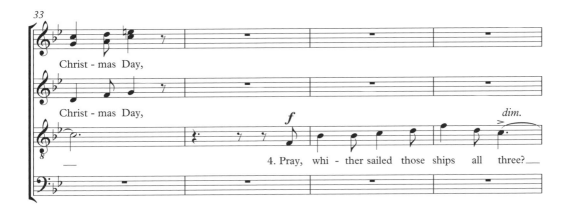

68

Man.

61

Christ-mas Day in the morn - ing.

ding, dong.

ding, dong.

ding, dong._____ (solo stop)

66 **un poco sostenuto**

mf espress. *cresc.*

7. And all the an-gels in heav'n shall sing, On Christ-mas Day, on Christ-mas Day, And

mf espress. *cresc.*

7. And all the an-gels in heav'n shall sing, On Christ-mas Day, on Christ-mas Day, And

mf espress. *cresc.*

7. And all the an-gels in heav'n shall sing, On Christ-mas Day, on Christ-mas Day, And

mf espress. *cresc.*

7. And all the an-gels in heav'n shall sing, On Christ-mas Day, on Christ-mas Day, And

un poco sostenuto

71 *ten.* **a tempo** *p*

all the an-gels in heav'n shall sing, On Christ-mas Day in the morn - ing.

ten. *p*

all the an-gels in heav'n shall sing, in the morn - ing.

ten. *p* *f*

all the an-gels in heav'n shall sing, in the morn - ing. 8. And

ten. *p* *f*

all the an-gels in heav'n shall sing, in the morn - ing. 8. And

Commissioned by the Guildford Festival 1973

Let all the world in every corner sing

George Herbert (1593–1632)　　　　　　　　　　Grayston Ives (b.1948)

God, my God and, my

God, my God and, my

God, my God and, my

God, my God and, my

God and King!

God and King!

God and King!

God and King!

Gt. to Ped. off